THIS JOURNAL
BELONGS TO:

_____

_____

_____

Poetry Journal

INSPIRATION:

TYPE OF POEM:

- HAIKU
- FREE VERSE
- TANKA

- SONNET
- EPITAPH
- CINQUAIN

- BLANK VERSE
- LIMERICK
- SESTINA

WORKING TITLES:

_____

_____

_____

WORKING THEMES:

_____

_____

_____

SUBMITTED TO:

_____

_____

_____

_____

_____

PUBLISHED:

_____

_____

_____

_____

_____

PROMPTS

- Write about seasons of change.
- Write about overcoming heartbreak.
- Write about a recent dream.
- Write about a fear you want to conquer.
- Write about a present goal you want to accomplish.
- Write about solitude.
- Write about a major change in your life.
- Write about something that makes you happy.
- Write about a song that reminds you of your childhood.
- Write a haiku about the moon.
- Write a haiku about time travel.
- Write a haiku about the weekend.
- Write about the first sound you hear in the morning.
- Write a poem about a personal achievement.
- Write a blackout poem about your current mood.
- Write about your first love.
- Write about something that disappointed you.
- Write about a time you should have stood your ground.
- Write about the smell of each season.
- Write about being late.
- Write about being lost in a foreign country.
- Write about volunterring at a nursing home.
- Write about leaving home.
- Write about your most treasured possession.
- Write a losing someone you loved.
- Write about procrastination.
- Write about a time you had to humble yourself.

POETRY STARTERS

1. stillness	26. irrelevant
2. connected	27. hidden beauty
3. windowless room	28. soap box
4. letting go	29. unplugged
5. explore	30. intuition
6. coffee	31. renewal
7. loyalty	32. spaceship
8. betrayal	33. hibiscus
9. peace	34. revolution
10. doubt	35. centered
11. elevate	36. glue
12. blue	37. weird vibes
13. text message	38. broken clock
14. rumors	39. drenched
15. breaking the rules	40. rose petals
16. rain water	41. lost love
17. elegance	42. resilient
18. miracles	43. approached
19. audacity	44. whispers
20. flawed	45. infatuated
21. omit	46. grateful
22. presentable	47. warm embrace
23. cloudy afternoon	48. fearless
24. intense	49. midnight
25. superpower	50. bloom

POETRY STARTERS

1. chandelier
2. tweet
3. hidden message
4. sunset
5. bully
6. shade
7. poisonous
8. bridge
9. bad grade
10. touch
11. scream
12. rescued
13. apology
14. wish
15. winter blues
16. restoration
17. value
18. laughter
19. longing
20. gratitude
21. rage
22. amused
23. liberosis
24. attachment
25. aubade

26. heliotrope
27. stressed
28. skyscraper
29. hazel
30. curve
31. seat belt
32. primrose
33. sweet
34. anchor
35. vice
36. hero
37. sillage
38. querencia
39. obscure
40. authentic
41. savage
42. anecdoche
43. lace
44. pride
45. bravery
46. plains
47. boxed in
48. adventure
49. river
50. permission

POETRY STARTERS

-WRITE YOUR OWN STARTERS-

1.

2.

3.

4.

5.

6.

7.

8.

9.

10.

11.

12.

13.

14.

15.

16.

17.

18.

19.

20.

21.

22.

23.

24.

25.

Poetry Journal

INSPIRATION:

TYPE OF POEM:

- HAIKU
- FREE VERSE
- TANKA

- SONNET
- EPITAPH
- CINQUAIN

- BLANK VERSE
- LIMERICK
- SESTINA

WORKING TITLES:

_____

_____

_____

WORKING THEMES:

_____

_____

_____

SUBMITTED TO:

_____

_____

_____

_____

_____

PUBLISHED:

_____

_____

_____

_____

_____

POETRY STARTERS

-WRITE YOUR OWN STARTERS-

1.

2.

3.

4.

5.

6.

7.

8.

9.

10.

11.

12.

13.

14.

15.

16.

17.

18.

19.

20.

21.

22.

23.

24.

25.

Poetry Journal

INSPIRATION:

TYPE OF POEM:

- HAIKU
- FREE VERSE
- TANKA

- SONNET
- EPITAPH
- CINQUAIN

- BLANK VERSE
- LIMERICK
- SESTINA

WORKING TITLES:

_____

_____

_____

WORKING THEMES:

_____

_____

_____

SUBMITTED TO:

_____

_____

_____

_____

_____

PUBLISHED:

_____

_____

_____

_____

_____

POETRY STARTERS

-WRITE YOUR OWN STARTERS-

1.
2.
3.
4.
5.
6.
7.
8.
9.
10.
11.
12.
13.
14.
15.
16.
17.
18.
19.
20.
21.
22.
23.
24.
25.

Poetry Journal

INSPIRATION:

TYPE OF POEM:

- HAIKU
- FREE VERSE
- TANKA

- SONNET
- EPITAPH
- CINQUAIN

- BLANK VERSE
- LIMERICK
- SESTINA

WORKING TITLES:

_____

_____

_____

WORKING THEMES:

_____

_____

_____

SUBMITTED TO:

_____

_____

_____

_____

_____

PUBLISHED:

_____

_____

_____

_____

_____

POETRY STARTERS

-WRITE YOUR OWN STARTERS-

1.

2.

3.

4.

5.

6.

7.

8.

9.

10.

11.

12.

13.

14.

15.

16.

17.

18.

19.

20.

21.

22.

23.

24.

25.

Poetry Journal

INSPIRATION:

TYPE OF POEM:

- HAIKU
- FREE VERSE
- TANKA

- SONNET
- EPITAPH
- CINQUAIN

- BLANK VERSE
- LIMERICK
- SESTINA

WORKING TITLES:

_____

_____

_____

WORKING THEMES:

_____

_____

_____

SUBMITTED TO:

_____

_____

_____

_____

_____

PUBLISHED:

_____

_____

_____

_____

_____

POETRY STARTERS

-WRITE YOUR OWN STARTERS-

1.
2.
3.
4.
5.
6.
7.
8.
9.
10.
11.
12.
13.
14.
15.
16.
17.
18.
19.
20.
21.
22.
23.
24.
25.

Poetry Journal

INSPIRATION:

TYPE OF POEM:

- HAIKU
- FREE VERSE
- TANKA

- SONNET
- EPITAPH
- CINQUAIN

- BLANK VERSE
- LIMERICK
- SESTINA

WORKING TITLES:

_____

_____

_____

WORKING THEMES:

_____

_____

_____

SUBMITTED TO:

_____

_____

_____

_____

_____

PUBLISHED:

_____

_____

_____

_____

_____

POETRY STARTERS

-WRITE YOUR OWN STARTERS-

1.

2.

3.

4.

5.

6.

7.

8.

9.

10.

11.

12.

13.

14.

15.

16.

17.

18.

19.

20.

21.

22.

23.

24.

25.

Poetry Journal

INSPIRATION:

TYPE OF POEM:

- HAIKU
- FREE VERSE
- TANKA

- SONNET
- EPITAPH
- CINQUAIN

- BLANK VERSE
- LIMERICK
- SESTINA

WORKING TITLES:

_____

_____

_____

WORKING THEMES:

_____

_____

_____

SUBMITTED TO:

_____

_____

_____

_____

_____

PUBLISHED:

_____

_____

_____

_____

_____

POETRY STARTERS

-WRITE YOUR OWN STARTERS-

1.

2.

3.

4.

5.

6.

7.

8.

9.

10.

11.

12.

13.

14.

15.

16.

17.

18.

19.

20.

21.

22.

23.

24.

25.

Poetry Journal

INSPIRATION:

TYPE OF POEM:

- HAIKU
- FREE VERSE
- TANKA

- SONNET
- EPITAPH
- CINQUAIN

- BLANK VERSE
- LIMERICK
- SESTINA

WORKING TITLES:

_____

_____

_____

WORKING THEMES:

_____

_____

_____

SUBMITTED TO:

_____

_____

_____

_____

_____

PUBLISHED:

_____

_____

_____

_____

_____

POETRY STARTERS

-WRITE YOUR OWN STARTERS-

1.
2.
3.
4.
5.
6.
7.
8.
9.
10.
11.
12.
13.
14.
15.
16.
17.
18.
19.
20.
21.
22.
23.
24.
25.

Poetry Journal

INSPIRATION:

TYPE OF POEM:

- HAIKU
- FREE VERSE
- TANKA

- SONNET
- EPITAPH
- CINQUAIN

- BLANK VERSE
- LIMERICK
- SESTINA

WORKING TITLES:

_____

_____

_____

WORKING THEMES:

_____

_____

_____

SUBMITTED TO:

_____

_____

_____

_____

_____

PUBLISHED:

_____

_____

_____

_____

_____

POETRY STARTERS

-WRITE YOUR OWN STARTERS-

1.

2.

3.

4.

5.

6.

7.

8.

9.

10.

11.

12.

13.

14.

15.

16.

17.

18.

19.

20.

21.

22.

23.

24.

25.

Poetry Journal

INSPIRATION:

TYPE OF POEM:

- HAIKU
- FREE VERSE
- TANKA

- SONNET
- EPITAPH
- CINQUAIN

- BLANK VERSE
- LIMERICK
- SESTINA

WORKING TITLES:

WORKING THEMES:

SUBMITTED TO:

PUBLISHED:

POETRY STARTERS

-WRITE YOUR OWN STARTERS-

1.

2.

3.

4.

5.

6.

7.

8.

9.

10.

11.

12.

13.

14.

15.

16.

17.

18.

19.

20.

21.

22.

23.

24.

25.

Poetry Journal

INSPIRATION:

TYPE OF POEM:

- HAIKU
- FREE VERSE
- TANKA

- SONNET
- EPITAPH
- CINQUAIN

- BLANK VERSE
- LIMERICK
- SESTINA

WORKING TITLES:

_____

_____

_____

WORKING THEMES:

_____

_____

_____

SUBMITTED TO:

_____

_____

_____

_____

_____

PUBLISHED:

_____

_____

_____

_____

_____

POETRY STARTERS

-WRITE YOUR OWN STARTERS-

1.
2.
3.
4.
5.
6.
7.
8.
9.
10.
11.
12.
13.
14.
15.
16.
17.
18.
19.
20.
21.
22.
23.
24.
25.

Poetry Journal

INSPIRATION:

TYPE OF POEM:

- HAIKU
- FREE VERSE
- TANKA

- SONNET
- EPITAPH
- CINQUAIN

- BLANK VERSE
- LIMERICK
- SESTINA

WORKING TITLES:

_____

_____

_____

WORKING THEMES:

_____

_____

_____

SUBMITTED TO:

_____

_____

_____

_____

_____

PUBLISHED:

_____

_____

_____

_____

_____

POETRY STARTERS

-WRITE YOUR OWN STARTERS-

1.
2.
3.
4.
5.
6.
7.
8.
9.
10.
11.
12.
13.
14.
15.
16.
17.
18.
19.
20.
21.
22.
23.
24.
25.

Poetry Journal

INSPIRATION:

TYPE OF POEM:

- HAIKU
- FREE VERSE
- TANKA

- SONNET
- EPITAPH
- CINQUAIN

- BLANK VERSE
- LIMERICK
- SESTINA

WORKING TITLES:

_____

_____

_____

WORKING THEMES:

_____

_____

_____

SUBMITTED TO:

_____

_____

_____

_____

_____

PUBLISHED:

_____

_____

_____

_____

_____

POETRY STARTERS

-WRITE YOUR OWN STARTERS-

1.

2.

3.

4.

5.

6.

7.

8.

9.

10.

11.

12.

13.

14.

15.

16.

17.

18.

19.

20.

21.

22.

23.

24.

25.

Poetry Journal

INSPIRATION:

TYPE OF POEM:

- HAIKU
- FREE VERSE
- TANKA

- SONNET
- EPITAPH
- CINQUAIN

- BLANK VERSE
- LIMERICK
- SESTINA

WORKING TITLES:

_____

_____

_____

WORKING THEMES:

_____

_____

_____

SUBMITTED TO:

_____

_____

_____

_____

_____

PUBLISHED:

_____

_____

_____

_____

_____

POETRY STARTERS

-WRITE YOUR OWN STARTERS-

1.

2.

3.

4.

5.

6.

7.

8.

9.

10.

11.

12.

13.

14.

15.

16.

17.

18.

19.

20.

21.

22.

23.

24.

25.

Poetry Journal

INSPIRATION:

TYPE OF POEM:

- HAIKU
- FREE VERSE
- TANKA

- SONNET
- EPITAPH
- CINQUAIN

- BLANK VERSE
- LIMERICK
- SESTINA

WORKING TITLES:

WORKING THEMES:

SUBMITTED TO:

PUBLISHED:

POETRY STARTERS

-WRITE YOUR OWN STARTERS-

1.

2.

3.

4.

5.

6.

7.

8.

9.

10.

11.

12.

13.

14.

15.

16.

17.

18.

19.

20.

21.

22.

23.

24.

25.

Poetry Journal

INSPIRATION:

TYPE OF POEM:

- HAIKU
- FREE VERSE
- TANKA

- SONNET
- EPITAPH
- CINQUAIN

- BLANK VERSE
- LIMERICK
- SESTINA

WORKING TITLES:

_____

_____

_____

WORKING THEMES:

_____

_____

_____

SUBMITTED TO:

_____

_____

_____

_____

_____

PUBLISHED:

_____

_____

_____

_____

_____

POETRY STARTERS

-WRITE YOUR OWN STARTERS-

1.

2.

3.

4.

5.

6.

7.

8.

9.

10.

11.

12.

13.

14.

15.

16.

17.

18.

19.

20.

21.

22.

23.

24.

25.

Poetry Journal

INSPIRATION:

TYPE OF POEM:

- HAIKU
- FREE VERSE
- TANKA

- SONNET
- EPITAPH
- CINQUAIN

- BLANK VERSE
- LIMERICK
- SESTINA

WORKING TITLES:

_____

_____

_____

WORKING THEMES:

_____

_____

_____

SUBMITTED TO:

_____

_____

_____

_____

_____

PUBLISHED:

_____

_____

_____

_____

_____

POETRY STARTERS

-WRITE YOUR OWN STARTERS-

1.
2.
3.
4.
5.
6.
7.
8.
9.
10.
11.
12.
13.
14.
15.
16.
17.
18.
19.
20.
21.
22.
23.
24.
25.

Poetry Journal

INSPIRATION:

TYPE OF POEM:

- HAIKU
- FREE VERSE
- TANKA

- SONNET
- EPITAPH
- CINQUAIN

- BLANK VERSE
- LIMERICK
- SESTINA

WORKING TITLES:

WORKING THEMES:

SUBMITTED TO:

PUBLISHED:

POETRY STARTERS

-WRITE YOUR OWN STARTERS-

1.

2.

3.

4.

5.

6.

7.

8.

9.

10.

11.

12.

13.

14.

15.

16.

17.

18.

19.

20.

21.

22.

23.

24.

25.

Poetry Journal

INSPIRATION:

TYPE OF POEM:

- HAIKU
- FREE VERSE
- TANKA

- SONNET
- EPITAPH
- CINQUAIN

- BLANK VERSE
- LIMERICK
- SESTINA

WORKING TITLES:

_____

_____

_____

WORKING THEMES:

_____

_____

_____

SUBMITTED TO:

_____

_____

_____

_____

_____

PUBLISHED:

_____

_____

_____

_____

_____

POETRY STARTERS

-WRITE YOUR OWN STARTERS-

1.

2.

3.

4.

5.

6.

7.

8.

9.

10.

11.

12.

13.

14.

15.

16.

17.

18.

19.

20.

21.

22.

23.

24.

25.

Poetry Journal

INSPIRATION:

TYPE OF POEM:

- HAIKU
- FREE VERSE
- TANKA

- SONNET
- EPITAPH
- CINQUAIN

- BLANK VERSE
- LIMERICK
- SESTINA

WORKING TITLES:

_____

_____

_____

WORKING THEMES:

_____

_____

_____

SUBMITTED TO:

_____

_____

_____

_____

_____

PUBLISHED:

_____

_____

_____

_____

_____

POETRY STARTERS

-WRITE YOUR OWN STARTERS-

1.
2.
3.
4.
5.
6.
7.
8.
9.
10.
11.
12.
13.
14.
15.
16.
17.
18.
19.
20.
21.
22.
23.
24.
25.

Poetry Journal

INSPIRATION:

TYPE OF POEM:

- HAIKU
- FREE VERSE
- TANKA

- SONNET
- EPITAPH
- CINQUAIN

- BLANK VERSE
- LIMERICK
- SESTINA

WORKING TITLES:

_____

_____

_____

WORKING THEMES:

_____

_____

_____

SUBMITTED TO:

_____

_____

_____

_____

_____

PUBLISHED:

_____

_____

_____

_____

_____

POETRY STARTERS

-WRITE YOUR OWN STARTERS-

1.
2.
3.
4.
5.
6.
7.
8.
9.
10.
11.
12.
13.
14.
15.
16.
17.
18.
19.
20.
21.
22.
23.
24.
25.

Poetry Journal

INSPIRATION:

TYPE OF POEM:

- HAIKU
- FREE VERSE
- TANKA
- SONNET
- EPITAPH
- CINQUAIN
- BLANK VERSE
- LIMERICK
- SESTINA

WORKING TITLES:

_____

_____

_____

WORKING THEMES:

_____

_____

_____

SUBMITTED TO:

_____

_____

_____

_____

_____

PUBLISHED:

_____

_____

_____

_____

_____

POETRY STARTERS

-WRITE YOUR OWN STARTERS-

1.

2.

3.

4.

5.

6.

7.

8.

9.

10.

11.

12.

13.

14.

15.

16.

17.

18.

19.

20.

21.

22.

23.

24.

25.

Poetry Journal

INSPIRATION:

TYPE OF POEM:

- HAIKU
- FREE VERSE
- TANKA

- SONNET
- EPITAPH
- CINQUAIN

- BLANK VERSE
- LIMERICK
- SESTINA

WORKING TITLES:

_____

_____

_____

WORKING THEMES:

_____

_____

_____

SUBMITTED TO:

_____

_____

_____

_____

PUBLISHED:

_____

_____

_____

_____

POETRY STARTERS

-WRITE YOUR OWN STARTERS-

1.

2.

3.

4.

5.

6.

7.

8.

9.

10.

11.

12.

13.

14.

15.

16.

17.

18.

19.

20.

21.

22.

23.

24.

25.

Poetry Journal

INSPIRATION:

TYPE OF POEM:

- HAIKU
- FREE VERSE
- TANKA

- SONNET
- EPITAPH
- CINQUAIN

- BLANK VERSE
- LIMERICK
- SESTINA

WORKING TITLES:

_____

_____

_____

WORKING THEMES:

_____

_____

_____

SUBMITTED TO:

_____

_____

_____

_____

_____

PUBLISHED:

_____

_____

_____

_____

_____

POETRY STARTERS

-WRITE YOUR OWN STARTERS-

1.

2.

3.

4.

5.

6.

7.

8.

9.

10.

11.

12.

13.

14.

15.

16.

17.

18.

19.

20.

21.

22.

23.

24.

25.

Poetry Journal

INSPIRATION:

TYPE OF POEM:

- HAIKU
- FREE VERSE
- TANKA

- SONNET
- EPITAPH
- CINQUAIN

- BLANK VERSE
- LIMERICK
- SESTINA

WORKING TITLES:

_____

_____

_____

WORKING THEMES:

_____

_____

_____

SUBMITTED TO:

_____

_____

_____

_____

_____

PUBLISHED:

_____

_____

_____

_____

_____

POETRY STARTERS

-WRITE YOUR OWN STARTERS-

1.

2.

3.

4.

5.

6.

7.

8.

9.

10.

11.

12.

13.

14.

15.

16.

17.

18.

19.

20.

21.

22.

23.

24.

25.

Poetry Journal

INSPIRATION:

TYPE OF POEM:

- HAIKU
- FREE VERSE
- TANKA

- SONNET
- EPITAPH
- CINQUAIN

- BLANK VERSE
- LIMERICK
- SESTINA

WORKING TITLES:

_____

_____

_____

WORKING THEMES:

_____

_____

_____

SUBMITTED TO:

_____

_____

_____

_____

_____

PUBLISHED:

_____

_____

_____

_____

_____

POETRY STARTERS

-WRITE YOUR OWN STARTERS-

1.

2.

3.

4.

5.

6.

7.

8.

9.

10.

11.

12.

13.

14.

15.

16.

17.

18.

19.

20.

21.

22.

23.

24.

25.

Poetry Journal

INSPIRATION:

TYPE OF POEM:

- HAIKU
- FREE VERSE
- TANKA

- SONNET
- EPITAPH
- CINQUAIN

- BLANK VERSE
- LIMERICK
- SESTINA

WORKING TITLES:

WORKING THEMES:

SUBMITTED TO:

PUBLISHED:

POETRY STARTERS

-WRITE YOUR OWN STARTERS-

1.

2.

3.

4.

5.

6.

7.

8.

9.

10.

11.

12.

13.

14.

15.

16.

17.

18.

19.

20.

21.

22.

23.

24.

25.

Poetry Journal

INSPIRATION:

TYPE OF POEM:

- HAIKU
- FREE VERSE
- TANKA

- SONNET
- EPITAPH
- CINQUAIN

- BLANK VERSE
- LIMERICK
- SESTINA

WORKING TITLES:

_____

_____

_____

WORKING THEMES:

_____

_____

_____

SUBMITTED TO:

_____

_____

_____

_____

PUBLISHED:

_____

_____

_____

_____

POETRY STARTERS

-WRITE YOUR OWN STARTERS-

1.

2.

3.

4.

5.

6.

7.

8.

9.

10.

11.

12.

13.

14.

15.

16.

17.

18.

19.

20.

21.

22.

23.

24.

25.

Poetry Journal

INSPIRATION:

TYPE OF POEM:

- HAIKU
- FREE VERSE
- TANKA

- SONNET
- EPITAPH
- CINQUAIN

- BLANK VERSE
- LIMERICK
- SESTINA

WORKING TITLES:

_____

_____

_____

WORKING THEMES:

_____

_____

_____

SUBMITTED TO:

_____

_____

_____

_____

_____

_____

PUBLISHED:

_____

_____

_____

_____

_____

_____

POETRY STARTERS

-WRITE YOUR OWN STARTERS-

1.
2.
3.
4.
5.
6.
7.
8.
9.
10.
11.
12.
13.
14.
15.
16.
17.
18.
19.
20.
21.
22.
23.
24.
25.

Poetry Journal

INSPIRATION:

TYPE OF POEM:

- HAIKU
- FREE VERSE
- TANKA

- SONNET
- EPITAPH
- CINQUAIN

- BLANK VERSE
- LIMERICK
- SESTINA

WORKING TITLES:

_____

_____

_____

WORKING THEMES:

_____

_____

_____

SUBMITTED TO:

_____

_____

_____

_____

_____

PUBLISHED:

_____

_____

_____

_____

_____

POETRY STARTERS

-WRITE YOUR OWN STARTERS-

1.

2.

3.

4.

5.

6.

7.

8.

9.

10.

11.

12.

13.

14.

15.

16.

17.

18.

19.

20.

21.

22.

23.

24.

25.

Poetry Journal

INSPIRATION:

TYPE OF POEM:

- HAIKU
- FREE VERSE
- TANKA

- SONNET
- EPITAPH
- CINQUAIN

- BLANK VERSE
- LIMERICK
- SESTINA

WORKING TITLES:

_____

_____

_____

WORKING THEMES:

_____

_____

_____

SUBMITTED TO:

_____

_____

_____

_____

_____

PUBLISHED:

_____

_____

_____

_____

_____

POETRY STARTERS

-WRITE YOUR OWN STARTERS-

1.
2.
3.
4.
5.
6.
7.
8.
9.
10.
11.
12.
13.
14.
15.
16.
17.
18.
19.
20.
21.
22.
23.
24.
25.

Poetry Journal

INSPIRATION:

TYPE OF POEM:

- HAIKU
- FREE VERSE
- TANKA

- SONNET
- EPITAPH
- CINQUAIN

- BLANK VERSE
- LIMERICK
- SESTINA

WORKING TITLES:

_____

_____

_____

WORKING THEMES:

_____

_____

_____

SUBMITTED TO:

_____

_____

_____

_____

_____

_____

PUBLISHED:

_____

_____

_____

_____

_____

_____

POETRY STARTERS

-WRITE YOUR OWN STARTERS-

1.

2.

3.

4.

5.

6.

7.

8.

9.

10.

11.

12.

13.

14.

15.

16.

17.

18.

19.

20.

21.

22.

23.

24.

25.

Poetry Journal

INSPIRATION:

TYPE OF POEM:

- HAIKU
- FREE VERSE
- TANKA

- SONNET
- EPITAPH
- CINQUAIN

- BLANK VERSE
- LIMERICK
- SESTINA

WORKING TITLES:

WORKING THEMES:

SUBMITTED TO:

PUBLISHED:

POETRY STARTERS

-WRITE YOUR OWN STARTERS-

1.

2.

3.

4.

5.

6.

7.

8.

9.

10.

11.

12.

13.

14.

15.

16.

17.

18.

19.

20.

21.

22.

23.

24.

25.

Poetry Journal

INSPIRATION:

TYPE OF POEM:

- HAIKU
- FREE VERSE
- TANKA

- SONNET
- EPITAPH
- CINQUAIN

- BLANK VERSE
- LIMERICK
- SESTINA

WORKING TITLES:

_____

_____

_____

WORKING THEMES:

_____

_____

_____

SUBMITTED TO:

_____

_____

_____

_____

_____

_____

PUBLISHED:

_____

_____

_____

_____

_____

_____

POETRY STARTERS

-WRITE YOUR OWN STARTERS-

1.

2.

3.

4.

5.

6.

7.

8.

9.

10.

11.

12.

13.

14.

15.

16.

17.

18.

19.

20.

21.

22.

23.

24.

25.

Poetry Journal

INSPIRATION:

TYPE OF POEM:

- HAIKU
- FREE VERSE
- TANKA

- SONNET
- EPITAPH
- CINQUAIN

- BLANK VERSE
- LIMERICK
- SESTINA

WORKING TITLES:

_____

_____

_____

WORKING THEMES:

_____

_____

_____

SUBMITTED TO:

_____

_____

_____

_____

_____

PUBLISHED:

_____

_____

_____

_____

_____

POETRY STARTERS

-WRITE YOUR OWN STARTERS-

1.

2.

3.

4.

5.

6.

7.

8.

9.

10.

11.

12.

13.

14.

15.

16.

17.

18.

19.

20.

21.

22.

23.

24.

25.

Poetry Journal

INSPIRATION:

TYPE OF POEM:

- HAIKU
- FREE VERSE
- TANKA

- SONNET
- EPITAPH
- CINQUAIN

- BLANK VERSE
- LIMERICK
- SESTINA

WORKING TITLES:

_____

_____

_____

WORKING THEMES:

_____

_____

_____

SUBMITTED TO:

_____

_____

_____

_____

_____

PUBLISHED:

_____

_____

_____

_____

_____

POETRY STARTERS

-WRITE YOUR OWN STARTERS-

1.

2.

3.

4.

5.

6.

7.

8.

9.

10.

11.

12.

13.

14.

15.

16.

17.

18.

19.

20.

21.

22.

23.

24.

25.

Poetry Journal

INSPIRATION:

TYPE OF POEM:

- HAIKU
- FREE VERSE
- TANKA

- SONNET
- EPITAPH
- CINQUAIN

- BLANK VERSE
- LIMERICK
- SESTINA

WORKING TITLES:

_____

_____

WORKING THEMES:

_____

_____

SUBMITTED TO:

_____

_____

_____

_____

_____

PUBLISHED:

_____

_____

_____

_____

_____

POETRY STARTERS

-WRITE YOUR OWN STARTERS-

1.

2.

3.

4.

5.

6.

7.

8.

9.

10.

11.

12.

13.

14.

15.

16.

17.

18.

19.

20.

21.

22.

23.

24.

25.

Poetry Journal

INSPIRATION:

TYPE OF POEM:

- HAIKU
- FREE VERSE
- TANKA

- SONNET
- EPITAPH
- CINQUAIN

- BLANK VERSE
- LIMERICK
- SESTINA

WORKING TITLES:

_____

_____

_____

WORKING THEMES:

_____

_____

_____

SUBMITTED TO:

_____

_____

_____

_____

_____

PUBLISHED:

_____

_____

_____

_____

_____

POETRY STARTERS

-WRITE YOUR OWN STARTERS-

1.

2.

3.

4.

5.

6.

7.

8.

9.

10.

11.

12.

13.

14.

15.

16.

17.

18.

19.

20.

21.

22.

23.

24.

25.

Poetry Journal

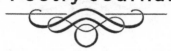

INSPIRATION:

TYPE OF POEM:

- HAIKU
- FREE VERSE
- TANKA

- SONNET
- EPITAPH
- CINQUAIN

- BLANK VERSE
- LIMERICK
- SESTINA

WORKING TITLES:

_____

_____

_____

WORKING THEMES:

_____

_____

_____

SUBMITTED TO:

_____

_____

_____

_____

_____

PUBLISHED:

_____

_____

_____

_____

_____

POETRY STARTERS

-WRITE YOUR OWN STARTERS-

1.

2.

3.

4.

5.

6.

7.

8.

9.

10.

11.

12.

13.

14.

15.

16.

17.

18.

19.

20.

21.

22.

23.

24.

25.

Poetry Journal

INSPIRATION:

TYPE OF POEM:

- HAIKU
- FREE VERSE
- TANKA

- SONNET
- EPITAPH
- CINQUAIN

- BLANK VERSE
- LIMERICK
- SESTINA

WORKING TITLES:

_____

_____

_____

WORKING THEMES:

_____

_____

_____

SUBMITTED TO:

_____

_____

_____

_____

_____

_____

PUBLISHED:

_____

_____

_____

_____

_____

_____

POETRY STARTERS

-WRITE YOUR OWN STARTERS-

1.

2.

3.

4.

5.

6.

7.

8.

9.

10.

11.

12.

13.

14.

15.

16.

17.

18.

19.

20.

21.

22.

23.

24.

25.

Poetry Journal

INSPIRATION:

TYPE OF POEM:

- HAIKU
- FREE VERSE
- TANKA

- SONNET
- EPITAPH
- CINQUAIN

- BLANK VERSE
- LIMERICK
- SESTINA

WORKING TITLES:

_____

_____

_____

WORKING THEMES:

_____

_____

_____

SUBMITTED TO:

_____

_____

_____

_____

_____

PUBLISHED:

_____

_____

_____

_____

_____

POETRY STARTERS

-WRITE YOUR OWN STARTERS-

1.

2.

3.

4.

5.

6.

7.

8.

9.

10.

11.

12.

13.

14.

15.

16.

17.

18.

19.

20.

21.

22.

23.

24.

25.

Poetry Journal

INSPIRATION:

TYPE OF POEM:

- HAIKU
- FREE VERSE
- TANKA

- SONNET
- EPITAPH
- CINQUAIN

- BLANK VERSE
- LIMERICK
- SESTINA

WORKING TITLES:

_____

_____

_____

WORKING THEMES:

_____

_____

_____

SUBMITTED TO:

_____

_____

_____

_____

_____

PUBLISHED:

_____

_____

_____

_____

_____

POETRY STARTERS

-WRITE YOUR OWN STARTERS-

1.
2.
3.
4.
5.
6.
7.
8.
9.
10.
11.
12.
13.
14.
15.
16.
17.
18.
19.
20.
21.
22.
23.
24.
25.

Poetry Journal

INSPIRATION:

TYPE OF POEM:

- HAIKU
- FREE VERSE
- TANKA

- SONNET
- EPITAPH
- CINQUAIN

- BLANK VERSE
- LIMERICK
- SESTINA

WORKING TITLES:

_____

_____

_____

WORKING THEMES:

_____

_____

_____

SUBMITTED TO:

_____

_____

_____

_____

PUBLISHED:

_____

_____

_____

_____

POETRY STARTERS

-WRITE YOUR OWN STARTERS-

1.

2.

3.

4.

5.

6.

7.

8.

9.

10.

11.

12.

13.

14.

15.

16.

17.

18.

19.

20.

21.

22.

23.

24.

25.